Dedications:

To the following people:

To all my sometime friends at Rankin Hall, University of Liverpool, wherever they are.

To Navtej Madhok, good friend, who makes damn all effort to contact me, but whom I love anyway.

To Steve and James, who find life difficult but who are good people nonetheless.

To Maggie and Bubba.

To my best waitresses who are Tamsin, Vicki, Carla and Camelia.

Bankers and poets.

Bankers work in banks
Because they want to get paid;
I want to get published
Because I want to get laid.

Written in 2010

Table of contents

Foreword

These poems and prose fragments were written over roughly twenty years, from the time when I was an undergraduate at Liverpool University in the early nineteen nineties until this year (2012). They are arranged in approximate chronological order as far as I can remember apart from 'Bankers and Poets.' The order is approximate because I did not date the poems at the time when I wrote them; the dates of the poems are thus very approximate, and indeed may in some cases even be mistaken. My two foreign language poems are in a separate section.

These poems and prose fragments, though not perhaps many considering they have been written over a twenty one year period, nevertheless represent a large portion of my creative output to date. I hope you enjoy them.

Memory of primary school.

When I was nine or ten,
I used to sit next to a boy at primary school,
A boy with square shoulders and cat's eyes.
Every morning,
When he came to sit down beside me,
He would hit me over the head.
I always used to ask him why he did it.
'Why?' he'd say,
'Because I fucking felt like it,
That's why.'

Even now, twelve or thirteen years later,
I think there's a part of me,
That dreams of killing him.

The other day,
I was standing in a bank,
Waiting to be served,
When a girl I knew came in.
'Oh God!' I overheard her saying,
'It's Toby.'
I stood there for a minute,
Wondering why it still hurt so much to be hated.
God knows, I've hated enough people in my time.

Written in 1991

1

Mother.

Mother, Mother,
You love me foolishly,
With your fifty-one year old grey hair,
And the smoke bubbling away in your lungs,
Like black magic.

Mother, mother,
You love me foolishly,
Because when I was eighteen,
I shouted at you,
And you thought
I was going to hit you,
And you ran upstairs,
Like a frightened hen.

Mother, Mother,
When you are dead,
In twenty or thirty years time,
I will bring flowers for your grave,
While I wait for death to come to me,
Thinking of you,
The only one stupid enough to love me.

Written in 1995.

Teddy bear.

In a high-ceilinged bedroom,
In a tall Dublin town house,
My teddy bear lies crying.
Twelve years ago,
When my half-sister was two,
And I was fifteen,
I gave him to her.
She was a sweet two year old,
My half-sister;
She used to kiss me awake
In the morning.
When I went back to England
After the holidays
She cried,
Because she missed me.
Sometimes I think I loved her,
Or might have loved her anyway.

Now, twelve years later,
She's obnoxious,
In the way only a fourteen year old could be.
She shouts at my father,
And ignores me,
And I certainly don't think
She gives a damn for my teddy.
I ought to go to Dublin,
Find my teddy
And say sorry to him,
But I don't think he'd understand.

Written in 1996.

A memory of Israel.

Red-eyed from heroin,
Bought as a present for her eighteenth birthday,
The beautiful Jewess led me,
Scruffy nineteen year old,
Through the streets of Tel Aviv
And told me I looked fine.

Later, in the apartment,
She was shy,
And went into the other room,
So I couldn't see her breasts
As she was dressing.

Oh my Jewess,
Perhaps tomorrow,
My life will begin again.
Because all down the dark years
I can still remember you,
Although you have forgotten
My face and my name.

Written in 1997

Memory of Saudi Arabia.

The boy's fat,
Like a toad,
And I'm pushing him
Through the door,
Into the headmaster's office.
And he doesn't hate me,
Because he's too frightened to hate me;
But I hate him.
He falls down,
And I try to pick him up
And push him through the door,
So that the headmaster can punish him,
And I have become what I hate.

Written in 1999.

The German teacher's retirement day.

I used to see you,
When I was thirteen or fourteen,
And you were coming up for sixty-five,
Throwing boys' school bags
Out of your classroom.
Though I didn't do German,
I knew you by reputation,
The most boring teacher in the school.

When you retired,
The headmaster gave you your present,
And you took it,
And smiled.

You knew it wasn't real of course;
You could feel our dislike,
Although we clapped dutifully,
If somewhat sarcastically.

Written in 2000

The serpent's words to Eve as she left the garden of Eden for the last time.

It was not I
Who taught sparrow
To heed hawk's cry,
As he wheeled on the wing
On fire in the sun.

It was not I
Who left Cain undone
As he wept on the morn,
As he woke from the storm
Which left his brother no more.

It was not I
Who left dusky woman to cry
As she watched her babe die,
As he struggled to find the light,
His by blesséd right.

It was not I
Who left the truth unsaid,
And forever perhaps unsayable;
When the vellum page was read
And the sack clothed men fled,
To wait for the time
When the knowledge burdened fool
Would finally come to rue
The words he had written
In his freshly printed book
After all forsook
The songs we had once loved
And known to be true.

It was not I
Who laughed
When the white-faced man
Sent the golden boys to die;
Oh death, come and catch as can,
In all the dirt and mud
Left behind from the flood

Which swallowed love and hope
Even the dead will surely choke
When the worms and maggots come
To swallow the remains
Of those we once cared for.

It was not I
Who ate the silver fruit
With the golden veined root,
Which in the garden grew
Where the fire tongued birds sang true
For you and your man;
In the garden where we played
Before we were afraid
Of the One who cast us out.

Written in 2000

Lecherous thoughts in the E.F.L. classroom, in Frankfurt, Germany.

The Turkish breasts come in juggling two by two;

I try to keep my mind on the grammar and my eyes off the view.

Oh sweet Turkish ladies please forgive me,

But I hope that your English stays bad;

Because if you ever understand this poem,

You're sure to get mad.

Written in 2001

For Anna K; meeting again after 7 years.

After seven long years,
Your eyes are full of tears.
Where have you been?
Who have you seen?
How was your luck?
Who did you fuck?
To be completely blunt,
Thinking of a guy's hands on your cunt,
Or his hands on your tits
Makes me feel like total shit.
You'll say 'You're being unfair.
How do you dare?
Aren't I free?
Doesn't my body belong to me?'
I know I'm being unfair,
But can't you see that I care?
In the end it doesn't matter where you've been
Or who you've seen,
Because you're still mean.
I should have known;
Why did I 'phone?

Just because I shouldn't feel something doesn't mean that I don't feel it.

Written in 2002

My mother and her cat - Carol and Pod.

My mother's old cat is slowly dying;
Cancer's eating away his stomach
And he won't stop crying.
'Twenty years for a cat,
He can't complain;
In our time together
He's been happy in the main.'
Twenty more years,
And she'll say the same;
'My life was a good one
And I can't complain;
I was happy in the main.'

Written in 2005

Poet's eyes

Wherever I go,
Bydgoszcz, Brescia or Guadalajara,
It's always the same -
On jest dziwny,
Tobias es un tipo muy raro,
Un po' strano, no.
People think I'm strange
Wherever I go;
'Though to myself
I'm as normal
As you are to yourself.

I saw a picture of myself
As a two year old child
Sitting on my father's knee.
My father was a well groomed
Handsome man
Of about twenty-eight,
Younger than I am now.

I was a beautiful child,
With blond hair;
But I can see even then,
That I had poet's eyes,
That went on and on,
Looking at nothing.

Written in 2005

Sunshine at Auschwitz,
rainy day in San Francisco.

Sunshine at Auschwitz, April 1944;
The Jew looks up and smiles.
True, the Russian tanks are still many months away,
(And in any case, if you aren't Jewish, the Russians on the whole
won't be much better than the other lot)
But it's a sunny day;
The commandant, instead of swearing or clipping him 'round the
ear as usual, slips him another half a potato.
Sunshine at Auschwitz.

Rain in San Francisco, April 2009;
The Jewess is sad.
She is twenty-four, with a Business degree from Stanford.
She enjoys bowling, tennis and sex with her non-Jewish boyfriend.
She thinks they might get married next year.
She's earning $90,000 a year;
This is a little better
Than most of her friends.
She goes into the bathroom,
Slits her wrists in the bath and waits.
Rain in San Francisco.

Written in 2005

13

Doha Blues - tefl rap.

Students here learn nothing

But I couldn't give a damn;

I'm just waiting to go home now,

And see my poor old mam.

They often say they hate me,

But I really couldn't care;

As far as I'm concerned,

Their hatred's quite unfair.

Their idiotic behaviour,

It often makes me mad;

But when I think what I might have been,

It makes me rather sad.

I could have been a lawyer,

On eighty grand a year,

With lots of pretty secretaries

And after hours beer.

In Rochester, there's snow now,

And beer upon the tap;

In Doha, it's hard to buy beer,

And it tends to taste like crap.

My pay isn't too bad,

And the sun is really hot,

But is this job worth doing?

It most certainly is not.

My colleagues don't really like me,

So much I fear is true;

My afternoons are lonely,

My social contacts few.

I'm just waiting to get out now,

And get my final pay,

I'm thirty-six years old now,

I feel like I'll be fifty in a day.

Written in 2005

The devil's ballad.

Dance, lady, dance
Beneath the apple trees,
On a summer evening,
With the bonfire smoking
And the summer birds a-keening.
For heart and soul will teach wisdom
When mind will not,
When the air is fragrant
And the embers grow hot
On a warm summer evening.
And soon, lady,
There will be no more time for dancing.
Yes, soon there will be no more time for dancing.
Hold your young man tight, lady,
Yes, hold him very tight;
All through the night, lady,
All through the warm summer night;
Because, soon, lady,
There will be no more time for dancing.
Yes, soon there will be no more time for dancing.
Forget the priests, lady,
Oh, forget the blessed priests;
For they have broken souls, lady,
Yes, they have broken souls.

And the church bell is mournful as it tolls,
Yes, the church bell is mournful as it tolls.
And soon there will be no more time for dancing,
Yes, soon there will be no more time for dancing.
And your beauty will soon be spent, lady,
Yes, your beauty will soon be spent.
And then there'll be no more time for dancing, lady,
Oh then there'll be no more time for dancing.

Written in 2005

Dead poets' society.

(After 'Tree Party' by Louis Macniece. Macniece was a contemporary of Auden, and, apart from Auden, was perhaps the most important British poet to emerge in the 1930s. The title is borrowed from the famous film of the same name with Robin Williams.)

Your health, Philip Larkin,
Despair grows deep,
Though wanking and sherry be cheap;
Philip the despairer,
Philip the sage,
Who was quite close to thirty
When he finally got laid.

Your health, W.H. Auden,
All will revere
W.H Auden the balladeer.
Wynstan the word player,
Wynstan the wit,
Wynstan who wrote copiously
But who never wrote shit.

Your health, William Yeats,
Among them all,
William B. Yeats stands at the fore.
William the rhymer,
William the great,
Whose characters fall in love,
But never masturbate.

Your health, Allen Ginsberg,
The howler of 'Howl'[1],
Shame that cancer grew in your bowl.
Allen the protester,
Allen the hip,
Who was fucked by pretty boys
And found governments shit.

Your health, T.S. Eliot,
April is cruel[2];
'Four Quartets'[3] is ever so cool.
Thomas the great thinker,
Thomas the stern,
Who could have fucked who he liked,
But was too taciturn.

Your health, Dylan Thomas,
I loved 'Fern Hill,'[4]
But you're so hard, it makes me ill;
Dylan the very difficult,
Dylan the flawed,
Who, loved by Taylor's[5] wife,
Was often impure.

Your health, Louis Macniece;
56 years[6],
So much hope, so many tears;
Louis loved his Latin[7],
Louis taught Greek,
Pretty students bent over,
Down their blouses he'd peek.

Written in 2005

[1] Ginsberg's most famous poem was called 'Howl'
[2] See 'The Wasteland' by T.S. Eliot.
[3] Apart from 'The Wasteland' Eliot's most famous work.
[4] One of Dylan Thomas' two most famous poems.
[5] It is said that A.J.P. Taylor's wife was in love with Dylan Thomas. Taylor, as everyone knows, was a very famous British historian.
[6] Macniece died aged 56 of pneumonia.
[7] Macniece taught classics at the University of Birmingham.

The death of my tortoise.

In the evenings
The daddy long-legs buzzed.
My tortoise was small and green,
And, at the age of six,
He was the best present I'd ever had.
And when my sister picked him up,
He looked like an old man.
I loved my tortoise.
When I found him for the last time,
In late September,
His eyes had gone
And he was as dead as dead can be.
I sat on my mother's knee and bawled.
The tears lacerated my face like knives.
Twenty-one years later,
When my father tried and failed to kill himself,
It never hurt as much.

Written in 2005

The death of Pan Dumbrowski.

(Pan is Polish for 'mister'.)

As Mr. Cancer ran laughing,
Through his body,
Spreading up from his arse,
He stared into his wife's eyes
As he gasped and gasped.
He knew then that he had never loved her at all,
And, as for his faith,
It fell out of his body
And splattered on the floor.
He would have struck her if he could,
But Mr. Cancer had given him limbs of wood.
He would have cursed her if he could,
But Mr. Cancer had given him a tongue of wood.

Written in 2005

Old crimes

(Gorbachev, as everyone knows, was leader of the Soviet Union between 1985 and 1991. He did not graduate from university until 1955, two years after Stalin's death. It is highly improbable that he was in any way connected with the monstrous crimes of the Stalinist era, although he did join the Communist party while still a student (I am not sure quite when, if after or before Stalin's death), so his career as a Communist and Stalin's may be said to have overlapped. Perhaps he denounced people to the secret police. Perhaps he threatened to do so, in order to gain a material advantage over others. You never, as they say, really know. In so far as I have a political hero, Gorbachev is mine, although I also hold Nelson Mandela in high regard. On the other hand, he rose to power during the time of Khrushchev and Brezhnev; although the Soviet Union was not as bad under them as under Stalin, it still was, compared to Britain and the U.S.A., in the 1950s and 1960s, a fairly morally repugnant place. I suspect (although maybe it's just jealousy because I've never been in charge of anything) that to go high in any organisation, you have to be prepared to lie, cheat and betray and, sadly, I think even such figures as Gorbachev and Mandela are probably not exempt from this law . As George Orwell said, 'Saints should be presumed guilty until found innocent.' Incidentally, although I find many things to admire about Gorbachev, I understand that among Russians he is often loathed because he is held as being responsible for the demise of the Soviet Union and the Russians' consequent loss of superpower status. More people living in Russia today probably admire Stalin than Gorbachev, although Stalin was far more of a monster than Gorbachev is. Living within a system and having personal experience of it is no guarantee that you will understand it better than those who do not live within it. In fact, I think, with regard to Stalin, the reverse is true - we in the West have a more realistic view of Stalin than the Russians do themselves.)

Far, far back,
Far as memory goes,
Blood still trickles through Siberian snow.
The iron mouth opened wide,
Lovers were lost in the crimson tide.

Gorbachev, Gorbachev,
What do you know
Of Stalin's missing millions
Beneath the snow?

Far to the north,
The wolves still howl,
When shall we the truth allow?
In their beds at night,
The very old still cry
Who shall dare to ask them why?

Gorbachev, Gorbachev,
What do you know
Of Stalin's missing millions
Beneath the snow?

Written in 2009

The only homophobe in England.

(This piece is inspired by the poem 'To see the rabbit' by Alan Brownjohn. I know very little about Alan Brownjohn, but I like this poem and there is a lot of information about him on the net, including the full details of the aforementioned poem. My own piece imagines a future world which is at once very tolerant and, paradoxically, peculiarly totalitarian. A woman takes her children to the zoo to educate them against wicked prejudices like homophobia.)

Down the elevator,

Into the tube,

Past the billboards on either side;

We're going on a trip, kids,

To see the last homophobe in England.

They keep him in a cage at London Zoo.

When you arrive,

It's sunny and there are big crowds,

And you can see him –

An old, white, moustachioed, man,

With old-fashioned glasses,

And (horror of horrors) a cigarette in his mouth!

Although it's sunny

You have to take the kids home,

Because the crowd is in an ugly mood.

'Why can't you be more tolerant?'

Says a pretty young woman with red hair.

'Why can't you see that we lesbians are just the same as everyone else? If only you were a little more tolerant, we would gladly let you go?'

'Why can't you be more tolerant?' the crowd begins to howl.

'Why can't you just learn a little more tolerance?' they howl.

A young man picks up a small stone, and, with a skilful throw through the cage bars, manages to hit the last homophobe on the cheek; a small bloody rivulet appears on his cheek, just beneath his eye.

Realising that he is in danger yet again,

The last homophobe retreats into his den at the back of the cage.

Inside, there is his stack of girly magazines; the government doesn't really approve of such things, but still lets you have them if you pay enough money or if you are an important organisation like London Zoo.

He tries to masturbate, but aged sixty-three, he is really too old for that. He thinks of his one child, a daughter, and her one child, a son; and knows he will not see them again, because they will not face the hostile crowds, and he does not really blame them? Who, after all, wants to see her father's daily humiliation? He remembers the gay pride march into the zoo last year; thousands of men and women with whistles shouting death threats into his cage; the zoo, as a special favour, let them stay until midnight. He often hopes he will die before the one this year.

He consoles himself as always that he will die a martyr to his beliefs, although he is sad, because he knows that homophobia will die with him.

Outside, the crowd begins its familiar chant –

'What do we want? Freedom from prejudice! When do we want it? Now!'

He knows it will last for a couple more hours, until at 8 pm the zoo shuts.

Written in 2009.

The clown and the wives of Bydgoszcz.

For Anna Olkiewicz.

(Bydgoszcz is a town in Poland where I lived for three years between 1995 and 1998.)

The clown accepts laughter with a smile on his face,
But in his secret heart, he hates the one who laughs at him.
The wives of Bydgoszcz go to church
Because they want to go to heaven,
But in their secret hearts
They know that heaven is a lie.

The clown might be saved
By the warm summer air at night,
Which smells of flowers and is full of the sound of crickets.
He might even learn to stop being a clown,
But the wives of Bydgoszcz will never be saved.

Written in 2009

Wish to be taller.

(I'm five foot five and a half and will probably shrink with age. I blame it on my Jewish ancestry.)

How I wish, how I wish
That I were six foot four;
But at my age,
I'm unlikely to grow much more.

Written in 2009

I don't know, child, I don't know.

Why does the crow peck at the lamb's eyes?
Why does the crow peck at the lamb's eyes?
I don't know, child, I don't know.

Why does the man put his cigarettes on his daughter's arm?
Why does he put them on her arm?
I don't know, child, I don't know.

Why does the policeman hit the woman in front of her four year old
daughter?
Why does he hit her in front of her four year old daughter?
I don't know, child, I don't know.

Why does the cat make the mouse scream?
Why does the cat make the mouse scream?
I don't know, child, I don't know.

Why are the weasel's teeth so red?
Why are the weasel's teeth so red?
I don't know, child, I don't know.

Where does the night go?
Where does the night go?
I don't know, child, I don't know.

Where will the stars go?
Where will the stars go?
I don't know, child, I don't know.

Written in 2010

Francesca and Circe- a ballad.

(Francesca was an Italian girl of twenty-one whom I met some years ago. To this day, I think she is probably the most beautiful girl I have ever met. Circe was a mythological figure, an immortal sea goddess who imprisoned Odysseus on her island for a year because she was in love with him. I knew a very beautiful twenty-one year old American girl once, with long natural blond hair and brown eyes. She is perhaps the second most beautiful girl I have ever met (although I can think of others who would come close.) For the purposes of this poem, I have envisaged her as Circe.)

Francesca, Francesca,
Of all the most fair,
With her icy blue eyes,
And cascading black hair.

Francesca, Francesca,
With the icy blue eyes,
Who lay with her lover
Beneath azure skies.

Circe, Circe,
Who came from the sea,
Who rescued lost sailors
And forever was free.

Circe, Circe,
With your long yellow hair,
Apart from Francesca
By far the most fair.
Circe, Circe,
Forever be free,
Making love with lost sailors
From beyond the sea.

Francesca, Francesca,
Your face will grow old,
Your beauty will shrivel
And your heart grow cold.

Circe, Circe,
You'll forever be young,
Making love with lost sailors
Beneath the evening sun.

Circe, Circe,
Oh please shed a tear
For Francesca the beautiful
Who was without peer.

Francesca, Francesca,
Who was past compare.
Not even a sea goddess
Was ever as fair.

Written in 2010

Languages.

Polish is made of silver,
Latin is made of gold;
Italian is good for declaring love,
But English leaves me cold.

Written in 2010

Love song for a lady too young for me.

I find nocturnal noises oddly soothing;
The far away sound of adolescent anger,
And farther still, the fox's cry.
The passing years have not made me wealthy,
And yet here I am safe from frost and fire,
Safe from the hard tongued boys who once did me wrong.
Here their cruelty cannot find me;
In my flat I am safe from hunger and the rain.

Yet, lady, I wish that you lay beside me,
With your black hair draped upon my shoulder,
Your naked breast heaving softly,
Tired after lovers' tryst.

Though lady, I am by far your elder,
Yet I would save you from the rain,

Save you from the pain of a younger man
Who one day will no longer want you,
Save you from the fierce ingratitude of children loved.

Written in 2010.

Ask the boy who pulls the wings off sparrows.

Ask the boy who pulls the wings off sparrows,
Ask the spider in her web,
Ask the drunkard with the needle in her arm,
Ask them what the old man said.

Ask the boy who pulls the wings off sparrows,
Ask him what the old man said,
Ask the baby in her cradle,
Ask the man whose hands are red.

Ask the beggar who killed the blind man,
Ask him what the old man said.
Ask the politician to whom lies come easy,
Ask him what the old man said.

Ask the man who was so hungry;
Ask him what the old man said.
Ask the boy who raped the child,
Ask him what the old man said.

Ask the little girl who watched the man beat her mother;
Beaten by a rod of lead;
Who cried and wept
But could do nothing,
Ask her what the old man said.

Written in 2010.

Toby's summer in Rochester, Kent, England.

(After 'Kraj Majales', by Allen Ginsberg).

May is too beautiful to last more than a month;

June will come with a bump.

July will be warm,

But I bet the days will be grey;

And I've no money for a week's holiday.

In August, French exchange students are a real pain;

Then, before you know it,

It's the fucking autumn again.

Written in 2011

Polish children's prayer to Josef Stalin.

(In 1939-40, the Soviet Union and Nazi Germany shared out Poland between themselves. Russian commissioners visited schools in the Soviet sector and told little children to pray to God for bread. When it failed to appear, the commissioners told the children to pray to Josef Stalin; as a reward for having done so, they were given freshly baked bread rolls. In this way, the commissioners demonstrated to the children that Stalin was more powerful than God.)

Our Stalin,
Who art in Moscow,
Hallowed be thy name.
Thy kingdom come,
No sorry, the workers' paradise come,
The people's will be done,
In Poland as it is in Russia.

Gives us this day our daily bread,
And forgive us our trespasses,
As we forgive those who trespass against us,
Although we will never forgive anyone who trespasses against Thee,
Who art our Lord and Comrade Stalin.

Yes, please give us, Lord Stalin, our daily bread,
And if we are hungrier than little children in the U.S.A. and Britain,
That is only because British and American children are spoilt
capitalist brats, who have too much of everything,
Apart from the black slaves, who have nothing to eat at all.

We believe in thee, Lord Stalin,

And we will never believe wicked western smears,

Like the one which says that Lavrenti Beria[1] is a serial rapist and murderer

Or the one which says that, while the ignorant masses adore Thee,

everyone who knows Thee personally secretly hates thee,

But is too frightened to say so.

We love thee and believe in thee, Comrade Stalin,

And not in God the Father,

(Who is an invention of the bourgeois capitalist west).

Written in 2011

---

[1] Head of the N.K.V.D. (the Soviet secret police) under Stalin. Rumoured to have murdered Stalin to forestall Stalin murdering him

A holiday in the west of Ireland.

It was the golden time,
Before my sister had begun to wish that I didn't exist;
The poison that my grandmother had poured into me had not
begun to work yet.
My father's lover did not humiliate me as much as she was to later.
We loved the jellyfish which we found on the beaches,
And we believed that if we sang to the limpets on the rocks that
they would hear our songs.
I was eight perhaps;
She was nine or ten.
When we were playing outside the house where my father was with
his lover,
My sister said to me:
'If only we could be this age forever.'
It was only years later that I understood her.

Written in 2011

A riposte to Oscar Wilde's most famous quote *'We are all in the gutter, but some of us are looking at the stars.'*

(As you, gentle reader, no doubt know, Oscar Wilde was a famous aesthete and writer who was imprisoned for being a homosexual, and died at the end of the 19th century at a fairly young age. The above is the most famous of many pithy and witty statements attributed to him.)

'We are all in the gutter, but some of us are looking at the stars.'
No, Oscar;
Some of us are in the gutter, looking at the stars;
Others of us are in tenement blocks, dreaming of fast cars.

Some of us are in the gutter, looking at the stars;
Others of us are in Ferraris, undoing ladies' bras.

Written in 2011

Proust, Joyce and me.

No one really likes *Finnegan's Wake,*
Though some pretend they do;
But if you want real boredom
Try *A la Recherche du Temps Perdu.*

Oh critics have written reams about Joyce and Proust,
But about me they apparently don't give a shit.
It's not fair I say;
My verses are heartfelt and metrical,
And full of vim and wit.

Written in 2011

George Vault Blues

(After 'Bagpipe Music' by Louis Macniece)

For Camelia, Carla and Tamsin.

Camelia was in the ladies,
Messing with her make up;
'I really ought to marry,' she thought,
'My love life needs a shake up.
Back home in Bucharest,
Men are much more romantic;
Here they're always badly dressed,
With libidos far too frantic.'

Tamsin was in the kitchen,
Washing plates and glasses.
'That man looking at me is so fat,' she thought,
'You'd think he had two arses.
I'm sick of getting meagre tips
And old men's lecherous glances;
If they offered me a job in Bluewater,
I think I'd take my chances.'
Carla was in the backroom,
Counting up her money.
'I had too much to drink last night;
I'm feeling rather funny.
I'd better go home right now;
I'd better take a taxi;
I'd better tell the manager;
Let's hope he don't get waxy.'

Pete the barman stood on the bar,
And declared that he was sober;
He counted his feet to prove the fact,
And found he had one foot over.

It's no go the George Vaults
It's no go the casino;
I ought to read Shakespeare,
To improve my mind,
But instead I read 'The Beano';
I met a young lady in here who found out my age

And now she'll never see me;
I told Camelia I was twenty-two,
But I don't think she believed me.

Written in 2011

Here was the coin

For want of a nail, the kingdom was lost.

Here was the coin
Which made the waitress bend over
To give it back to the young man in the cafe
Who had dropped it.
Here was the waitress
Whose long blond hair and shapely breasts
Made the young man start speaking to her.
Here were the young man and the waitress
Who married each other.
Here was the marriage
Which made a baby.
Here was the baby
Who became a man.
Here was the man
Who had a loud voice.
Here was the loud voice
Which made young men love the loud-voiced man.
Here were the young men
Who made an army.

Here was the army
Which drenched the world in blood.
For want of a nail, the kingdom was lost.

Written in 2012

Susan in Narnia

A continuation of The Lion, The Witch and The Wardrobe

When the White Witch had been killed and Aslan had gone back to the magic place where he lived with his father The Emperor Overseas; Peter, Susan, Edmund and Lucy stayed to become the kings and queens of Narnia and lived there happily for many years.

Susan had been a little older than Lucy when the children first came to Narnia, twelve years old in fact, while Lucy was only nine. She enjoyed playing croquet with Lucy on the lawn of Cair Paravel, and practicing archery and the lessons she and the other children had with the centaurs, who taught the children the history of Narnia and botany and astronomy. The boys learned how to use weapons and horsemanship; Susan and Lucy were taught how to tend the sick by the beautiful dryads, and also learned archery and horse riding.

Sometimes, though, she found Lucy a little childish; after all, there is quite a big difference between nine and twelve, and she didn't always feel very close to her brothers either. However, she loved spending time with the beautiful dryads, who are tree spirits; she visited them in their houses, which are little huts next to the trees whose souls they share.

Already, before she had come to Narnia, Susan had noticed some small brown hairs growing between her legs; she asked Silennooth, the dryad, about them, and Sillennooth told her that she shouldn't worry and that all dryads and daughters of Eve had them, and that it just meant she was growing up.

One day, when she was going to sleep in her beautiful four poster bed, she felt wrenching pains in her stomach, and a little while later blood came from the hole between her legs. She was scared, so she called one of her dryad handmaidens to her, called Selene. Selene helped bathe her, and explained how dryads and river gods made babies, and said it was what the daughters of Eve and sons of Adam did as well. She said it was Aslan's way of making new people come into Narnia, and told her that soon she would want to do that with a man or a river god too. She said that Susan shouldn't lie with a man until she was at least seventeen or Aslan would be angry. Then Selene taught her how to put a piece of silk in the secret place between her legs and how it would catch the blood every month. Selene also told her that if she wanted to lie with a man or river god and not make a baby, then she must wash vinegar between her legs, but that she was too young for such things.

Three years passed and Susan was happy, happier than anyone in our world could be. There was no pain, no hunger and no injustice in Narnia, and there were no bills to pay. She began to look at the young men who came from faraway lands, and if they were handsome, she used to think about them as she rubbed between her legs. She talked to them and nodded pleasantly, but she remembered what Selene had said and never kissed them.

In her bedroom she had a big picture of Aslan and sometimes, when she was thinking about the young men and rubbing between her legs, she fancied that the lion's eyes were glaring at her.

That summer was a golden one. There was jousting on the lawns, and Susan won an archery competition against her handmaidens. One day, men came from Calormen to talk to Peter about selling fruit from Calormen which you couldn't grow in Narnia easily - dates and figs and so on. Susan was not interested in boring things like trade agreements, but she was a well brought up young girl and knew she had to be polite to the proud and courteous men with whom her brothers spoke. There were five of them and she met them all and curtsied when they bowed to her. The youngest was a tall, slim young man called Ashalleen. She liked the way his muscles rippled under his shirt and his deep brown eyes. He was a wonderful shot with a bow as well.

There was a banquet that evening and she made sure that Ashalleen sat beside her. He was as grave and courteous as the rest, but his eyes sparkled when he looked at her. She asked him to come and look at the chess set Mister Tumnus the faun had given her which was in her private apartments in the palace. The chess set was made of a beautiful stone and they began to play. When they had finished, Ashalleen stood up and said he must leave, but Susan led him to her chamber and asked him to stay. She took off her gown, and the young man could see her delicious fifteen-year-old breasts. He kissed her lightly at first, but then savagely, and soon they were naked. As he entered her, she gasped in pain and stared at the portrait of Aslan on her wall; the lion's eyes glared angrily at her, but she did not care.

Written in 2012

Toby's conversation with God.

(This owes a fair amount to 'A History of the World in 10 ½ Chapters', 'A Hitch Hiker's Guide to the Galaxy', 'Memnoch the Devil' and 'The Riverworld Series'.

I would like to state that I have not written this piece with the intention of offending anyone. The point I am trying to make is that, even if God exists, the fact of his/her/its existence does not necessarily give answers to the most fundamental questions we can ask about our existence. I feel that a truly good, religious person would in any case forgive me for writing it. If you don't believe me about Mother Teresa, then I suggest you look on the web about Christopher Hitchen's investigation of her.)

Scene : I am eighty-five years old, and have had lung cancer for a few months. I am intermittently lucid, with a machine attached to me which makes a beeping noise, and which is monitoring my circulation and respiration. Suddenly, its beeping becomes irregular, and I breathe my last. I find myself in a black void .In the distance, a tall bearded man aged apparently about seventy appears; he is wearing white robes. He does not seem to be walking on anything and a vague radiance is coming from him. He looks rather like a restored Greek statue, is at a guess six foot four and is fairly distinguished looking.

Toby: Oh that's better, the pain's gone. Where am I?

God: You're dead.

Toby: Really, and who might you be?

God: I'm God.

Toby: Sorry?

God: I'm God. I am Allah, Yahweh, God the Father, Zeus, Jupiter, Krishna, you name it.

Toby: Weird. I've never had a dream like this before.

God: You aren't dreaming. You're dead.

Toby: How do I know I'm not dreaming?

God: Can you remember ever smelling anything in a dream? *(God produces in quick succession the smell of oranges, petrol and egg flavour farts.)*

Toby: You're God? No joke? Shit, am I going to hell? I never went to church. Anyway I can get out of going to hell? Is this the last judgement? Shit.

God *(laughs)*: Don't worry, you aren't going to hell. Nobody goes to hell. That's an invention. I never send anyone to hell, and that includes Mao, Hitler, Stalin and Jack the Ripper. Everyone goes to heaven. I feel I owe you lot that much. You can abuse me, swear at me, pick your nose in front of me, do whatever you like. You still get heaven. Have you ever read 'A History of the World in 10 and 1/2 chapters?' It's fairly accurate. Everyone, atheists included, gets heaven. I'm a merciful God. You can be tall and handsome, which I know you've always wanted to be, you can go to night clubs in London, and get off with girls and go home with them, which I know you've always wanted to do, instead of just looking at them, as you used to in your younger days. You will always be twenty-tree years old, you can do whatever you like with all the cute girls you used to know, including that cute nineteen year old girl in Mexico who I know you always liked but you never managed to so much as kiss. You can eat chocolate without getting fat, listen to Socrates discoursing, snort cocaine; you can even murder people if you like. I never judge. JUDGE NOT THAT THOU BE NOT JUDGED, that goes for me too. Of course, eventually you'll get bored and opt for oblivion, which I can also arrange, but you're a fairly resourceful fellow, and you like reading, so I'd give you a good 900 years or so.

48

Toby: So what's the point of meeting me here then?

God: I thought I'd give you a chance to ask all those questions you've always wanted to ask me.

Toby: Great. Trouble is, I don't know where to start.

God: *(laughs)* Don't worry, I've got all the time in the world. And I mean everything and anything; ask whatever you like. I won't be offended. As they say, I'm compassionate and merciful.

Toby: Right, for a start, who are you? The Muslim one? The Christian one? Or to put the question another way, who was right?

God: I'm not really any of them; all human cosmologies are wrong.

Toby: So Jesus wasn't your son? You didn't breathe life into Mary's womb? Jesus doesn't sit at your right hand?

God: No, to repeat, all human cosmologies are wrong.

Toby: I have another question. How can you be talking to me? There must be loads of people dying at approximately the same time as me. Do you talk to them as well?

God: I can exist simultaneously for different people.

Toby: And you made everything, right?

God: The observable universe, yes.

Toby: Next obvious question: what were you doing before you made the universe?

God: Hanging around in the void masturbating.

Toby: Masturbating? You have sex organs then?

God: I'm male.

Toby: Interesting. Next question. What made you?

God: I don't know. All I remember is being here in blackness.

Toby: So you are eternal? You have, as it were, always existed?

God: I don't know. I have no memory of being created, but that's not to say it didn't happen. I just don't know.

Toby: And there are things outside you and outside the universe which you created?

God: I don't know. I think there probably are, at least I hope there are, but I really don't know. The thought that everything begins and ends with me seems fairly terrible to me.

Toby: You don't seem to have the answers any more than I do!

God: I don't. I'm sorry, people are always disappointed in me when they meet me. As you suspected all along, the fact of my existence doesn't really solve any human dilemmas.

Toby: Fucking hell, I kind of always knew it would be like this.

God: I'm sorry.

Toby: Well there are some more questions I'd like to ask you anyway.

God: Fire away.

Toby: Why did you create the universe?

God: Well, I was in the void, nothing was around me, I began masturbating, and I fashioned my seed into the galaxies. I did it out of boredom.

Toby: Before we go any further, let me remember a conversation I once had with an Anglican priest. He once posited the same question: what was God doing before the creation? The only sensible answer we could come up with was this: God couldn't have existed before the creation because there would have been no time and space for Him to exist in. The question is therefore nonsensical. How can you have existed before the universe? What did you exist in?

God: Your logic is sound, I have thought about this myself; it makes me suspect that I was created. However, I have no memory of being created. All I can remember is being in a black void.

Toby: Can you move? Outside the universe I mean?

God: Yes, I can, but wherever I go, there's just endless blackness.

Toby: Sounds depressing.

God: Yeah, it is. That's why I created the universe, and why I spend so much time watching it.

Toby: And how many worlds have intelligent life on them?

God: Fewer than you'd think, considering the size of the universe, only a few thousand or so.

Toby: And how similar are these intelligent beings to us humans?

God: Physically, I made you vary a lot; there are big ones and little ones, blue ones, green ones and purple ones. On the other hand, the laws of science apply everywhere and intelligent beings everywhere have pretty much the same intellectual capacity as you humans do; people everywhere have the same ideas about right and wrong; on all planets, for example, it's wrong to steal. I always split intelligent beings into two sexes.

Toby: Where exactly is heaven in the universe?

God: I built it next to the universe. Oh yes, and before you ask, it can't be seen by intelligent life in the universe.

Toby: So moral laws are constant throughout the universe?

God: Yes.

Toby: Lying is wrong everywhere?

God: Yes.

Toby: Why?

God: I don't know. I think I have the same ideas about right and wrong you have.

Toby: Why?

God: I don't know. Again, this makes me suspect that I am a created being, and I was imbued with a moral sense by whatever created me.

Toby: Here's the old philosophical saw. 1. God is all good. 2. God is all powerful. 3. There is injustice in the world (or for that matter in the universe.) These propositions don't square. What do you say to that?

God: I wouldn't claim to be either all good or all powerful.

Toby: You aren't all powerful?

God: No, sorry, I'm not.

Toby: What limits are there to your power?

God: I can't create new universes. *(He smiles ruefully)* I can't masturbate anymore. Why that should be, I have no idea.

Toby: Could you destroy the universe?

God: No, I can't. At a pinch, I can destroy the odd star system, but the whole damned thing seems to have run away from me. It's like a baby which got too big.

Toby: Can you intervene in our world? Miracles and such like?

God: Yes, I can, but I tend not to. In the whole of human history, I've only done it once. That was Moses and the burning bush. I've learned not to, by trial and error on other planets.

Toby: Most people in our world seem to have a pretty bad time.

God: (smiles ruefully) Intelligent life has a bad time pretty well everywhere in the universe.

Toby: Couldn't you have made life a little happier? What about all the innocent babies who die every day in Africa?

God: I never said I was all good. I'm a games player. On the other hand, I give all intelligent life heaven after death.

Toby: Intelligent life? What about animals and plants? Do they go to heaven too?

God: Higher animals, that is mammals, reptiles and amphibians do. Insects, plants and microbes don't.

Toby: Seems a fairly arbitrary delineation.

God: It is, I never claimed to be all good. Then, again, heaven's only got so much space.

Toby: What about the big bang?

God: A local phenomenon. And before you ask, it doesn't happen on my say so. It's just a periodic local phenomenon.

Toby: How much of the universe can humans actually see?

God: Only a very small part.

Toby: Will humans be able to see the whole universe before the next big bang?

God: No.

Toby: Will we ever have contact with intelligent life on other planets?

God: Yes, you lot are due for contact with two races. I reckon in about a thousand years or so. But you'll find it disappointing. Things aren't so different elsewhere.

Toby: So Einstein was wrong? Light speed is not an insuperable barrier?

God: Well, you're no physicist. The best answer I can give to a layman like you is both yes and no.

Toby: Hmmm... I'm trying to think about what else to ask you. Can I meet you again after I go to heaven?

God: I can give you two more appointments before you opt for oblivion. Everyone opts for oblivion in the end.

Toby: Why only two? I thought you said you could exist simultaneously for different people?

God: I can, but as I've already told you, I suspect my power is not infinite, which is why I limit everyone to three appointments: one immediately after death, and two more at any time before they opt for oblivion. Each appointment is limited to twenty-four hours. An arbitrary length of time, I know, but as I said before, I think my power is not infinite. I have to conserve it.

Toby: Do you think you could die?

God: I have no idea. I often wish I could. You humans are so fucking lucky you get oblivion. You should try existing in the void indefinitely.

Toby: I hate to say this, but you disappoint me.

God: As I've already said, everyone thinks that.

Toby: Hmmm... What else can I ask? Wait a second. O.k. here's one.

Catholics would say that evil is a question of human choice, that you are all good, and that the suffering of the innocent is a consequence of human choice.

God: *(laughs)* Sounds a bit thin, doesn't it? If I am all good, why should I let the innocent suffer? Why shouldn't I save them from their evil brothers and sisters? To be honest with you, I don't really buy the Catholic argument either. I suspect the universe is mechanistic, and that free will is an illusion. I can't be sure, 'though. The only defences I can offer is that I wouldn't say I was all good, and that all intelligent beings get a second chance.

Toby: How long have we been talking?

God: A couple of hours.

Toby: You said at the beginning of the conversation that we had all of the time in the world.

God: *(smiles)* That was an exaggeration. You've got twenty-two more hours.

Toby: You weren't lying about me going to heaven?

God: No.

Toby: Thank God for that. Sorry, slightly inappropriate remark.

God: Mafi mushskallah, as the Arabs might say.

Toby: Here's another question which has always puzzled me. How intelligent am I compared to other intelligent beings?

God: *(laughs)* Not as intelligent as you thought. You come in the top twenty percent or so.

Toby: *(Slightly indignant)* Come on! I learnt to speak nine languages. I had three novels and two collections of poetry published.

God: Yeah, but you were fairly lousy at maths. And you never made any money.

Toby: Who have you met who was a lot cleverer than me?

God: Oh, for fuck's sake, I've met Da Vinci, Einstein, Wittgenstein and Sartre!

Toby: Wittgenstein? Interesting. I was always fairly interested in Wittgenstein's philosophy, but never got 'round to reading it. Wasn't he the one who was interested in language? Whether words have intrinsic, absolute meaning or not?

God: Yes.

Toby: Do words have an absolute meaning, by the way?

God: Yes, but humans never know it.

Toby: Why not?

God: I prefer it that way.

Toby: Hmmm...Why don't you tell people you exist and that there is an afterlife? It would make everyone feel better, wouldn't it?

God: Yeah, but everyone's always disappointed in me. Plus the fact that it would reduce human life to an irrelevance, if everyone was sure it was a prelude to eternal happiness. It's come as a nice bonus to you, hasn't it? You always thought death was the end.

Toby: Did Wittgenstein and Sartre ask the same kind of questions as me?

God: Yes, but as they're a good deal more intelligent than you, their questions were rather more penetrating.

Toby: How good and kind am I relative to other intelligent beings?

God: *(laughs)* Slightly above average. You're no saint.

Toby: Are there any real saints?

God: Yes, but no famous people. You've got to be a bit of a shit to be famous. Apart from sportsmen and sportswomen, writers and actors and such

Toby: What about Mother Teresa?

God: A lying, mendacious bitch. Christopher Hitchens was dead right about her. She still got heaven, though.

Toby: I still wonder where you came from. Maybe we are just a small part of a macro verse. Maybe there is an infinite series of gods which create an infinite series of universes. A bit like an infinite series of smaller and smaller boxes.

God: Who knows? Your guess is as good as mine. I think what you really mean, is that you hope there is some sort of resolution to everything which will satisfy human intellect. I hope that too. I just don't know if there is one, 'though.

Toby: Hmmm... Let me think. There must be lots more things I can ask you. So, if I wanted to, I could spend my whole time raping and disembowelling young women?

God: Yes.

Toby: Surely the women themselves wouldn't want that if they're in heaven?

God: You would only be killing angels who would reconstitute themselves after you had finished with them.

Toby: There are angels?

God: Yes.

Toby: How many are there?

God: Billions and trillions and zillions. I made them out of my semen after I had finished creating the universe.

Toby: How different are they from us?

God: Like me, they are basically indestructible. They are, unlike me, totally selfless. They're my helpers.

Toby: What about Satan?

God: An invention.

Toby: I'm thinking, I'm thinking. You said animals got reincarnated?

God: Yes.

Toby: Cats and mice included?

God: All animals in heaven are vegetarian, including tigers and killer whales. Animals go on forever and never opt for oblivion. The savage garden isn't so savage in heaven. Animals can't reproduce 'though. It's to control the population. Humans can hunt simulacra of animals, but not the real animals, and all meat is artificially created by the angels.

Toby: There are certain individuals I would like to torture, like my mum's old boyfriend who threw me out of the house. Would I be able to torture him, as opposed to an angelic simulacrum of him?

God: No, but you could probably get to meet him, if he was agreeable to it, and he probably would be. Everyone mellows out in heaven in the end. When Adolph Hitler first came here, he spent his whole time chopping the heads off Jews and having sex with tall blond haired women. It took him a few years to work out they were only angelic simulacra. He's remarkably contrite now. When he isn't having sex, he spends his time painting, playing bridge and learning Hebrew.

Toby: Hitler studying Hebrew? Too weird.

God: *(laughs)* You said it.

Toby: Doesn't high technology exist in heaven? Physics and engineering and such like?

God: Yes.

Toby: Doesn't it worry you that evil dead souls might build sophisticated technology and conquer the universe and heaven?

God: There is a remarkable lack of mineral resources in heaven, including metal, which are necessary for building engines of war. Heaven's mostly orchards and beaches. Besides which, lots of angels are interested in high technology. They're always trying to find out if there's a macro verse, beyond my creation. They are, on the whole, about as intelligent as Da Vinci and Newton. Such an attempt could never happen, and would in any case be forestalled by angels.

Toby: A religious dictatorship of sorts.

God: *(laughs)* A theocracy in the truest sense.

Toby: Do people get to meet whoever they want in heaven?

God: Yes, provided the people they want to meet want to meet them. Otherwise, they just meet an angelic simulacrum.

Toby: Does bullying ever go on in heaven? I got picked on at school.

God: Any such incidents are nipped in the bud, and whoever is being bullied is replaced by an angelic simulacrum who can be bullied to the bully's heart's content.

Toby: Aren't there any dead people who nobody else can stand to be around?

God: Yes, they get looked after by angels, who have sex with them, or do whatever they want them to do.

Toby: I'm thinking. Who was the most intelligent person who ever lived?

God: Da Vinci.

Toby: Will anyone more intelligent than him ever be born?

God: Maybe. I can predict general trends for humanity, but I'm not so good with individuals. As I said, the universe in some ways has run out of my control.

Toby: Does it worry you that it'll ever run out of control completely?

God: Yes, that's why my angels are everywhere.

Toby: Who was greater - Proust or Joyce?

God: Proust.

Toby: Are men generally more intelligent than women?

God: No, but far more geniuses (you aren't one!) are men.

Toby: I've always liked modern history. Was American intervention in the First World War decisive?

God: Yes.

Toby: Which was the decisive battle of the Second World War?

God: Stalingrad.

Toby: Who was the greatest novelist of the twentieth century?

God: Mervyn Peake.

Toby: The greatest poet?

God: Yeats.

Toby: I've almost had enough. One final question 'though. I lived my life thinking there would be no after life. What prescriptions would you offer to a twenty-first century person who like me thought death was the end? I know it's a bit redundant now, but I'm still interested.

God: Lots of clichés: you have entered the city, so abide by its customs ,live for today, nothing to excess and don't expect to be happy. Oh, and try to be honest and generous. Nothing a primary school teacher couldn't tell the kids.

Toby: Okay, I'm ready.

God: Make a list of questions for next time.

(Scene changes. I'm still me, but I'm tall, very good looking and twenty-three. I find myself in a sunny orchard. I see a very pretty nineteen year old Mexican girl coming towards me.)

Toby: Hola, Veronica.

Veronica: Hola, Toby.

God: It may interest you to know she's not a simulacrum. She actually did fancy you when you were twenty-two, even though you were a short fat little git. You could have lived with her in Mexico, got married, and probably been happier than you were.

Toby: Never mind. I can't wait to kiss her! And do more besides!

Written in 2012.

Polacy i Anglicy.

My jesteś my polakami

Z krwią i z zołnierzami;

Wy jestescie anglikami,

Z morzem i z statkami.

Deszcz i wiatr,

To wasze,

Śnieg i mróz

To nasze.

My jesteśmy polakami,

Z wódką i z orgórkami;

Wy jestescie anglikami,

Z piwem i z truskawkami.

Ładne dziewczyny

To nasze,

Poważne pięniądze,

To wasze.

Torun i Kraków,

To nasze,

Oxford i Cambridge,

To wasze.

Łatwa historia,

To wasza;

Trudna historia,

To nasza.

Written in 2009

Love song in English and French.

Mademoiselle de vingt ans à peine,
Je voudrais que vous soyez la mienne.
Avec votre soutien-gorge de couleur rose
Qui tient étroit votre corps tout enclos.

Lady, if I could, I would pull down the sky for you;
For one night, maybe I would die for you.

Avec vos beaux cheveux si noirs,
Sans vos vêtements,
J'aimerais vous voir.
Avec votre visage et vos jolis seins;
Pour vous je pourrais écrire mille chansons.

Lady, if I could, I would pull down the sky for you;
For one night, maybe I would die for you.

Mais vous êtes si jeune
Que vous pourriez être ma fille;
Le passage du temps,
C'est la vie.

For one night, maybe I would die for you;
If I could, I would pull down the sky for you.

Written in 2012

Lightning Source UK Ltd.
Milton Keynes UK
UKOW040643030313

207054UK00001B/13/P